ISBN 978-0-9996326-4-2

The green sea turtle dips and dives
comes up for air, and then he spies
a little doll with shoes and socks
which were pulled out by a wave
and then caught in some rocks.

Where did that come from?
the sea turtle wondered.
Maybe the beach,
from the kids who have blundered.
They probably left
a few toys on the beach,
And now the sea took them
and they're out of reach.

Along came a blue plastic
shovel and pail,
and scooped up a slow moving,
beautiful snail.
The doll and the socks
went in it as well.
I do have one foot
said the snail as he fell,
but I don't need a sock or a shoe,
I can tell.

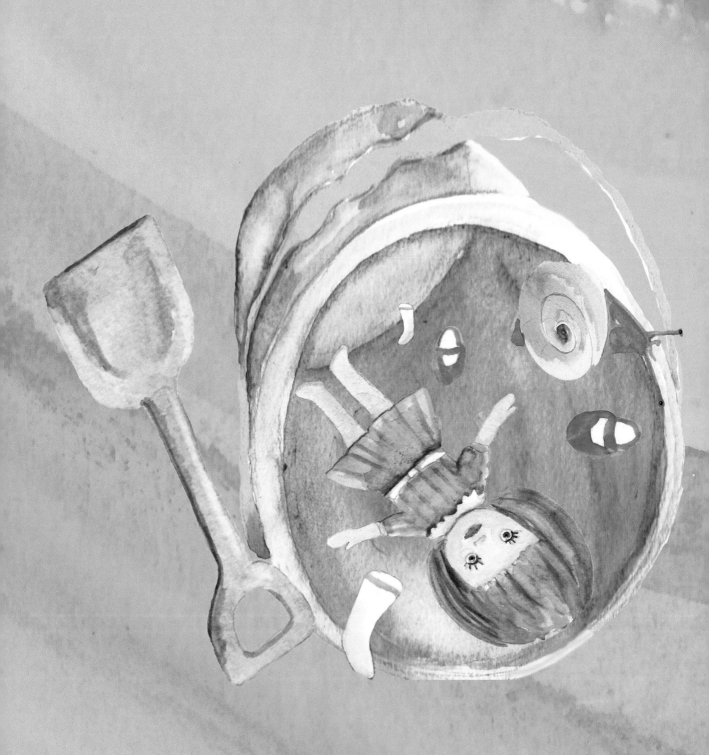

The pail and the shovel,
the doll and the snail,
continued to swirl
as if caught in a gale.

All of a sudden,
it caught something more,
a long moray eel
as it peeked out its door.

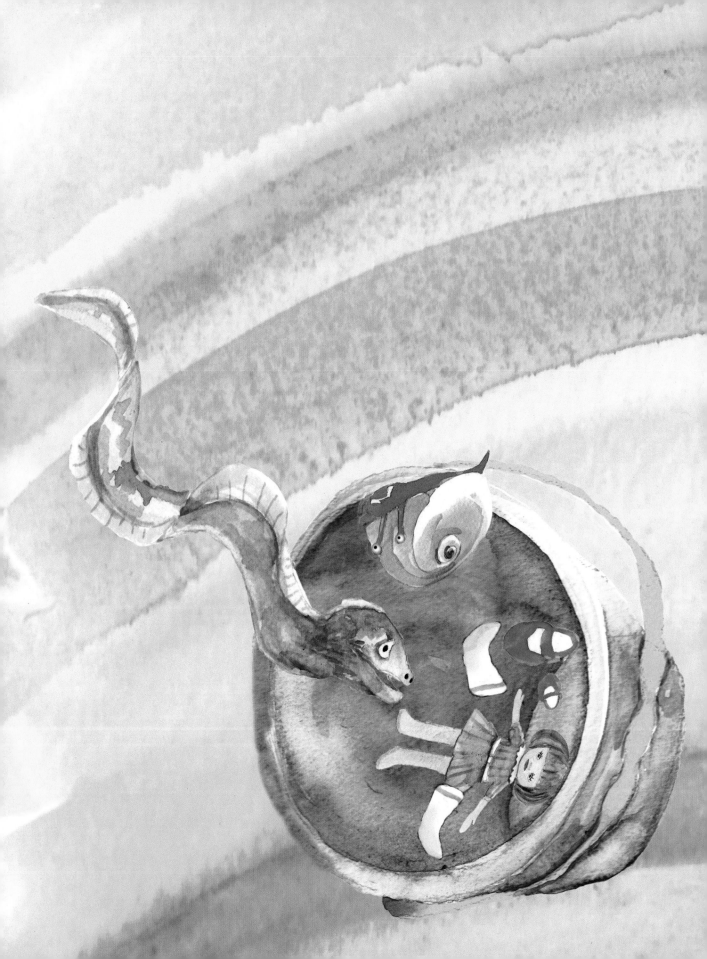

Well this is sure crazy,
the eel had to laugh.
Two socks and two shoes,
I don't even need half.
I have no feet at all,
and I don't like this pail.
Why are YOU here,
he asked the red snail.

It sure wasn't me who
planned this event.
We don't need these things
which the sandy beach sent.
The pail and the shovel,
the doll, snail and shoes,
and sea turtle following
this very long cruise,
then captured a sea horse
who was taking a snooze.

What happened to my safe
little harbor of kelp,
the seahorse said to the snail
with a yelp.

Hang on for the ride,
it is all you can do.
By the way, do you need
a sock or a shoe?

I don't think I do,
I have a tail.
I don't need a shovel,
or blue plastic pail.
The sea turtle tried to stop
all of the motion
of the crazy pail caught in
the big swirling ocean.

The handle was slippery,
moved a little too far,
dropped down to the sand
and scooped up a sea star.

I hope you might need
a doll, socks or shoes?
The snail hoped the sea star
would have some good news.
Not me said the sea star.
I do have five rays,
but I don't need them covered,
he said in a daze.

The sea horse, the snail,
the sea star and eel
went round and round like
the spokes on a wheel.
The pail gathered more,
there were three kinds of fish,
and the sea turtle then
made an important wish!

I wish that the kids on the beach
would pick up all of their stuff,
every fork, spoon and cup.
Every toy, every wrapper,
every straw, every cap,
we don't need the things
that end up in our lap.

I am going to save
my good friends in the pail,
which now has come close to
a krill eating whale!
What would happen if it got
into its mouth?
Would it come out the spout,
or head farther south?

The sea turtle tipped
the pail over just right.
The current was less,
to the creatures' delight.
They floated and swam back
to where they had come.
It wasn't a game
and it wasn't much fun.

Sea turtle then picked up
the sock and the shoe,
and found the doll in the sand
by a very small clue.
Back to the beach
he started to paddle,
and picked up a plastic pink
baby rattle.

Then he saw more of
the beach-goers' things,
tin cans and bags and soda pack rings.
Tennis balls, Frisbees, sandals galore,
how much could he find? There was
more and more!

Sea turtle got super charged after that,
and swam with the pail which
he wore like a hat.
He took the pail back to the kids
on the beach,
hoping a lesson to each he would teach.

He came up on the sand
to show them the trash.
The kids ran to the turtle
and saw in a flash,
that the pail was full of all
kinds of junk,
and the ocean doesn't need
all of that gunk!

The turtle soon left them
discussing the blight.
The kids then decided to
make it all right.
Each evening they could,
they would scan the beach,
for all of the trash which
was within reach.
They would tell other kids
to do more of the same, and
maybe could make it
a fun little game!

Sea creatures need
our complete attention,
to keep the place clean,
and not just a mention.
The message is clear -
we need no more plastic
in our home of the ocean -
help make it fantastic!

Did You Know?

Sea Turtles live all over the world where the ocean water is warm.

Eels are a type of fish and most live in shallow water.

Seahorses are very slow swimmers and live amongst seaweed.

Snails have been around for 500 million years, and can be land, ocean or fresh water types.

Sea stars used to be called starfish, but are not a fish at all, so the name was changed. Many sea stars have more than 5 rays.

Humpback whales have baleen instead of teeth. Baleen is like a comb which hangs from the roof of its mouth and collects krill. Krill is a small crustacean similar to tiny shrimp.

Kelp is a type of seaweed. Many ocean animals hide in the kelp forests, and also eat kelp. Seaweed is in many of our foods!

Blight can be anything that spoils or damages something. Trash and plastics in the ocean, lakes and streams hurt our land, water, and the animals.

Currents are the way water moves around, and are caused by many different things like the tides, sea floor, wind, and temperature.

Scan means *to look around*. Before you leave a park, stream, beach, yard, or school, you can scan the area and check to see if you left anything behind. If everyone picked up after themselves, the area would look nicer, and be safer for everyone and everything!

Leanne Roth resides in Southern California.
Working at a state beach as an
Interpretive Specialist, she has run the
Jr. Ranger program, campfire programs,
and many other events. She has noticed that
items are left abandoned on the beach,
and as the tide comes in and goes out,
the toys, sandals, hairbands, straws
and other things are pulled out to sea.

With her third book, "Sea Turtle's Wish," she
hopes to inspire young children (and everyone
else) to look around and pick up their things,
including trash.

Leanne also illustrated each of her books. She
enjoys using her artistic skills to design
interpretive panels, signs, logos, brochures and
fine art.

Made in the USA
Monee, IL
15 January 2023

25088003R00031